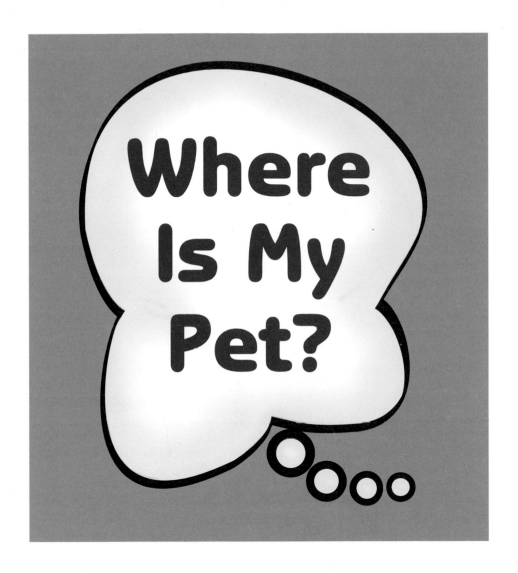

Where Is My Pet?

Written by Dawn Jacobs
Illustrated by Marion Elderidge

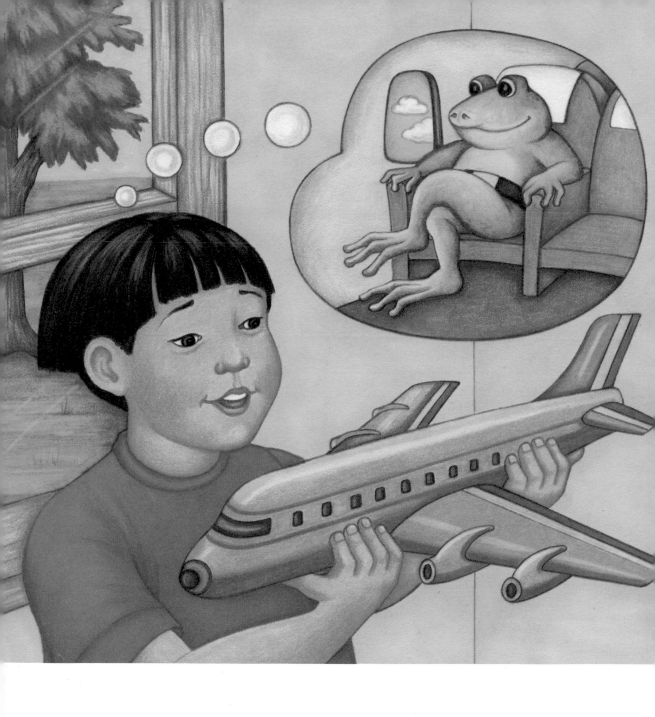

Is my pet in the jet?

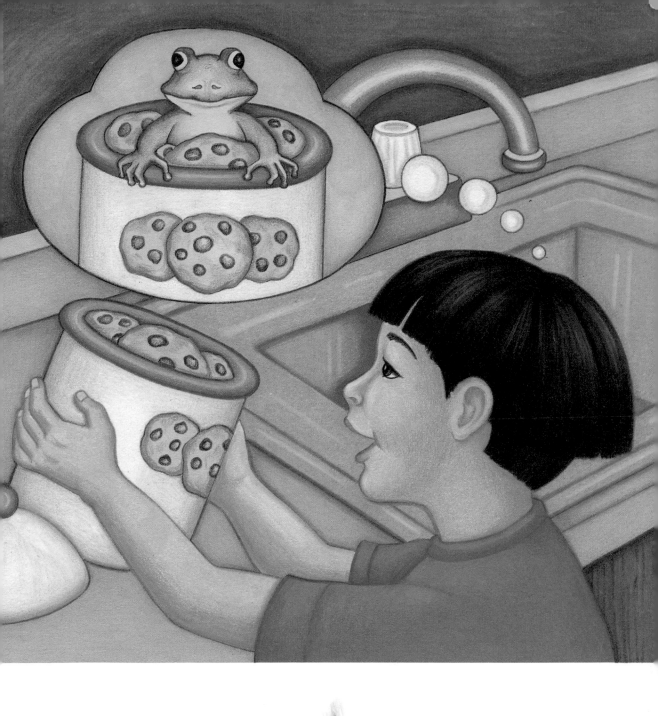

Is my pet in the jar?

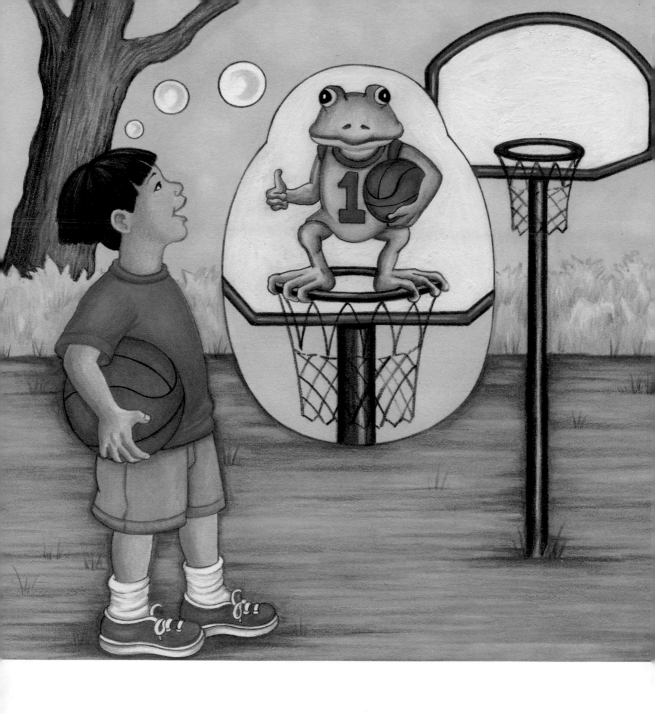

Is my pet on the net?

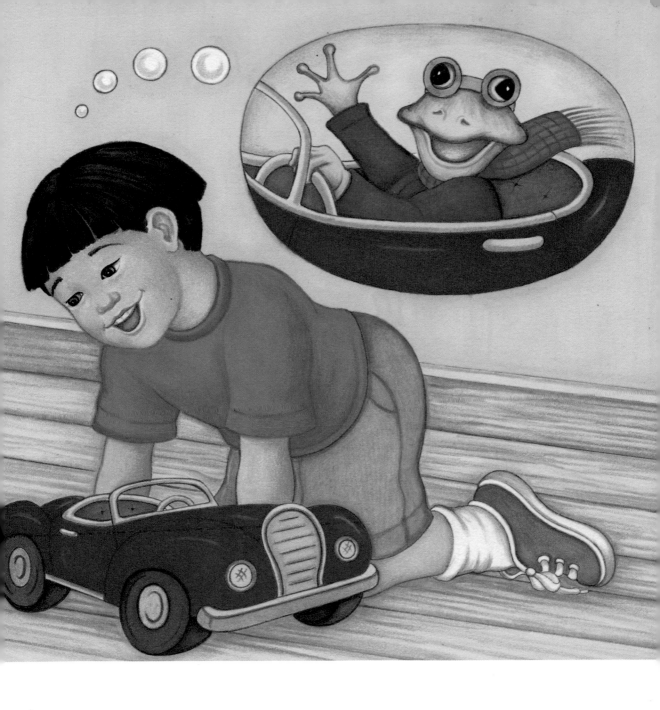

Is my pet in the car?

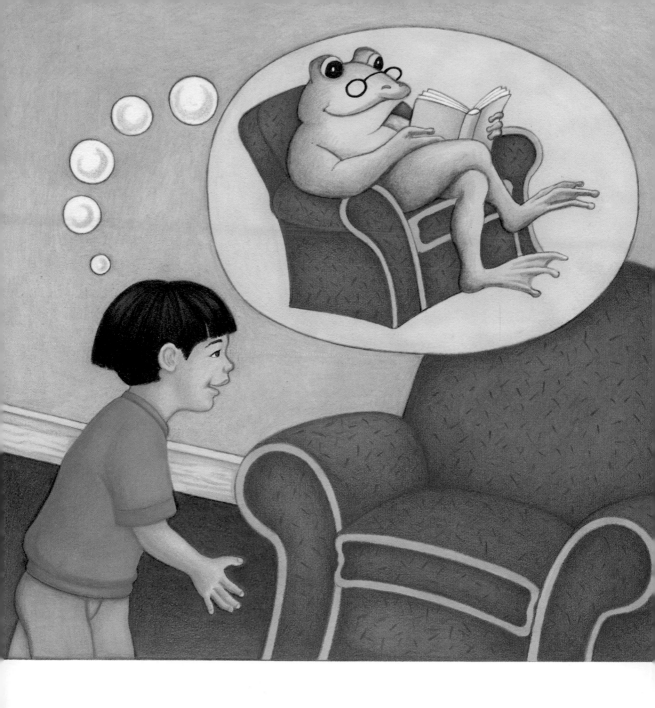

Is my pet in the chair?

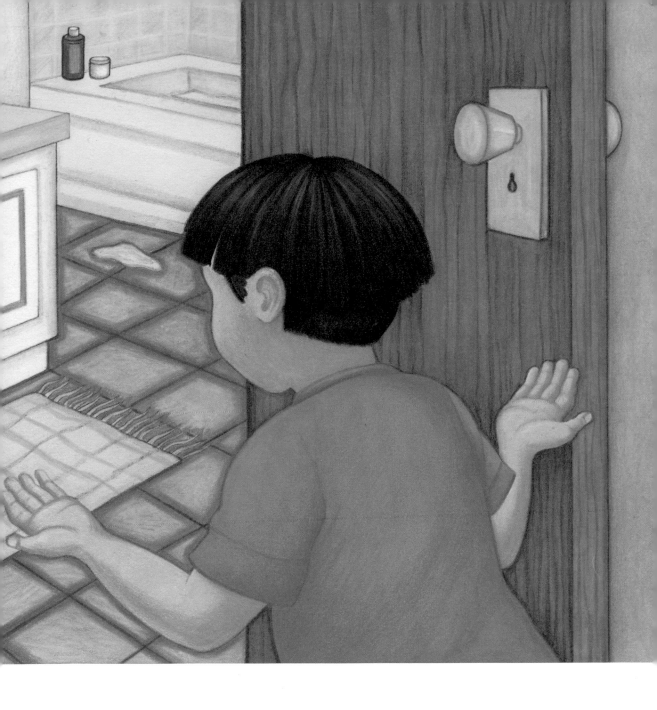

Where is my pet?

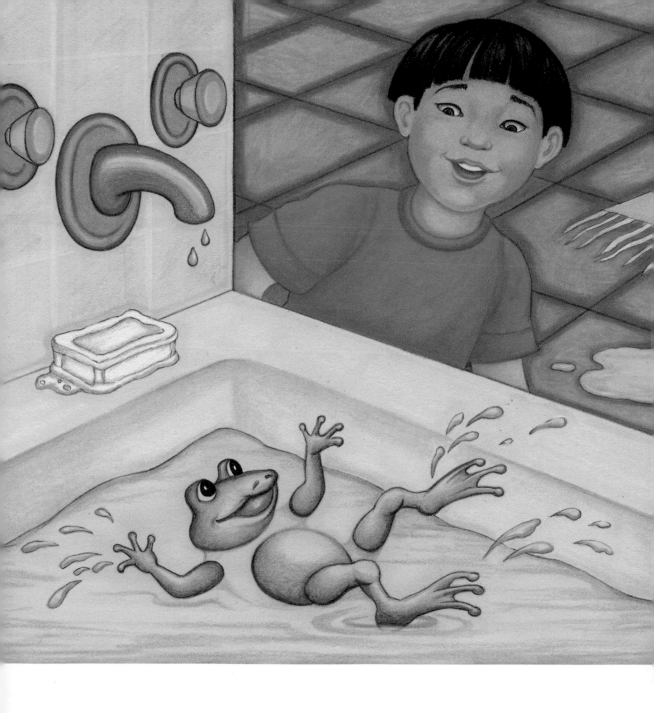

My pet is wet!